DIABETES
AND
God's Unending GRACE

DIABETES
AND
God's Unending GRACE

Pamela Diane (Vance) Worley

Copyright © 2024 by Pamela Diane (Vance) Worley.

All rights reserved. No part of this publication may be reproduced, distributed, or transmitted in any form or by any means, including photocopying, recording, or other electronic or mechanical methods, without the prior written permission of the copyright owner and the publisher, except in the case of brief quotations embodied in critical reviews and certain other noncommercial uses permitted by copyright law. For permission requests, write to the publisher, addressed "Attention: Permissions Coordinator," at the address below.

ARPress
45 Dan Road Suite 5
Canton MA 02021

Hotline: 1(888) 821-0229
Fax:　　1(508) 545-7580

Ordering Information:
Quantity sales. Special discounts are available on quantity purchases by corporations, associations, and others. For details, contact the publisher at the address above.

Printed in the United States of America.

ISBN-13:	Softcover	979-8-89389-144-7
	eBook	979-8-89389-143-0
	Hardcover	979-8-89389-145-4

Library of Congress Control Number: 2024914106

Table of Contents

Prologue vii

Chapter 1: A Rough Onset, December of 1965 1

Chapter 2: Diabetes Management Routine in 1965 5

Chapter 3 :High School Years as a Diabetic, 1965-1967 7

Chapter 4: First Year of College as a Diabetic, 1967-1968 9

Chapter 5: An Amazing Spiritual Transformation, September 22, 1967 .. 11

Chapter 6: A Christian University, 1968-1972 15

Chapter 7: Mobile, Alabama, 1975-1980 19

Chapter 8: Barber's Point, Hawaii, 1980-1983 21

Chapter 9: Elizabeth City, North Carolina, 1983-1990 23

Chapter 10: Our Sweet Little Baby from Seoul, Korea 25

Chapter 11: Back to Mobile, Alabama 29

Chapter 12: Home Sweet Home in Corpus Christi, Texas 31

Chapter 13: Would My Diabetes Allow Me to Teach? 33

Chapter 14:My First Seven Years of Teaching 37

Chapter 15: A Near Tragedy in 1999 41

Chapter 16: Teaching in the Corpus Christi I.S.D., 2000-2005 45

Chapter 17: An Unexpected Health Crisis in May of 2005 47

Chapter 18: An Educational Diagnostician for the Alice I.S.D. 49

Chapter 19: Teaching in the Lamar C.I.S.D. 51

Chapter 20: Teacher Retirement on January 15, 2012 55

Chapter 21: God's Wonderful Family 57

Chapter 22: A Leap of Faith 59

Chapter 23: Do You Know Your Eternal Destiny? 63

About the Author 67

Prologue

Hello, my name is Pamela Diane (Vance) Worley. I am sixty-nine years old, and I have had Type I Diabetes since diagnosed on December 4, 1965. Having begun my life journey as a diabetic at age fifteen, I hope this testimony will inspire you to obtain the most out of your insulin-dependent life that you possibly can.

Like the Apostle Paul in the New Testament of the Holy Bible, you also have a medical condition which you cannot eliminate. Theological discussion about Paul's incurable condition varies from a physical weakness to an incurable medical condition, disease, or whatever. But one thing is for sure as we read about Paul's petition to God for healing in 2 Corinthians 12:9-10. Paul was not healed because God had a higher purpose for him. Paul was to soon learn that God's grace was sufficient, and that God's strength would manifest itself through his infirmity or *thorn in the flesh*. Furthermore, Paul would glory in his infirmity because of the manifestation of Gods' power and strength through his weakness.

Never fear, I have no intention of either preaching to or discrediting you. But, I will be sharing what my Lord Jesus Christ has done in my heart and life.

Deep down inside, I know God allowed me to become a type 1 diabetic because he had a special plan for me. Through my diabetes, God has manifested his strength many times. His marvelous grace has met my every need. I give him all the glory and praise. I hope that my personal story will not only inspire you, but deepen your faith and trust in God. Perhaps you also will come to know Jesus Christ personally as your Lord and Savior. If you are a diabetic, God has you on a special assignment. He wants to manifest his strength and glory in you. I want you to discover blessings you could not have had otherwise without diabetes.

Chapter 1

A Rough Onset, December of 1965

I grew up in Iaeger, a small coal-mining town located in Southern West Virginia. In December of 1965, I was fifteen years old and in the eleventh grade at the town's only high school. I was a normal teenage girl and enjoyed playing trumpet in the high school band. I was also a local, district, and state leader in a Girl's Leadership Society. I had a passion for music, and had years of training on the piano. I made plans to pursue music as a career.

As early as the summer of 1965, while in summer band camp, I had brief moments of just not feeling well. I was thirsty all the time and drank lots water and sodas. Itching blisters had developed on both ankles. I attributed this to poison ivy. Thinking nothing was seriously wrong, I told no one. Fatigue began to bother me, and I felt tired all the time. My weight of approximately 138 pounds had begun to decrease slowly. Little did I realize, I had some classic signs of diabetes mellitus. I rejected the notion to tell anyone or to see a doctor.

Meantime, after school started in September, my usual lunch at school consisted of one bag of potato chips, one candy bar, and one soda drink.

By Thanksgiving of that year, I was feeling poorly most of the time. I had lost twenty-five pounds and continually drank sodas and water. On the evening of December 4, 1965, I attended a Sunday school party at our

Sunday school teacher's house. I remember lots of candy, nuts, mints, ice cream, pizza, and sodas. However, I didn't eat very much of these because I was starting to feel nauseated. I just sat on a couch and hoped the party would be over real soon.

My Sunday school teacher told me I didn't look well and perhaps was catching influenza. Her husband offered to take me home, and I accepted. When I got home, I threw up again and again. My parents finally returned home that evening and found black vomitus all over my bedroom floor. I had failed to make it to our bathroom in time. My mother speculated that I had perhaps gotten food poisoning from the pizza I had eaten. I didn't sleep that Saturday night because of repeated episodes of vomiting.

The next morning found me no better than before. My dad, fearing I would dehydrate, brought me a six sixteen ounce bottles of RC Cola, 7-Up, and Coke-a-Cola. Needless to say, the more I drank these sodas, the sicker I became. The high sugar levels in those drinks and in my blood were literally ending my life.

That late Sunday winter evening, I began having breathing difficulties.

My chest heaved up and down quickly as I gasped for air. Diabetes was almost unheard of in our small community. My mom and dad didn't suspect diabetes.

But, my struggling to breathe caused them to immediately drive to the nearest hospital over eighteen miles of hazardous ice-covered roads.

We were greeted by a hospital intern. He speculated that maybe I was pregnant and had too much to drink. How foolish! Because I was struggling to breathe, I was admitted to the intensive care unit at Grace Hospital in Welch, West Virgina. This was Sunday evening. I went into a full-blown diabetic coma shortly thereafter. My diagnosis was revealed to my parents by a doctor of internal medicine. He told mom and dad to not expect me to live because my blood sugar level tested a fatal high. The doctor told them that if I did survive, I would be advised to never bear children and that my life expectancy would maybe be twenty-five years at best.

I believe I woke up from the diabetic coma on either Tuesday or Wednesday. There, by my bedside, was mother's Methodist minister praying earnestly for my recovery. I will never forget this. I remained in the hospital for about ten days. I got back in time for the last day of school before Christmas vacation. Determined not to disappoint my band director, I elected to play my trumpet for the high school band concert that day.

The prognosis for my young life did not hold any promise, but I was determined it would. I wanted to finish college and begin my music career as a public-school music teacher. Deep down inside, even at the age of five, I knew that this was what I was supposed to do with my life. I shared with mom that I wanted to direct a high school band.

She replied, "Ah no, honey, you will teach music in elementary school."

Her third grade classroom was only one of many classrooms I visited to teach music during my junior and senior year of high school. I enjoyed this immensely. Besides, it became my perfect plan of escape from high school study hall. The elementary school was only a short walking distance from the high school.

Chapter 2

Diabetes Management Routine in 1965

Allow me to begin by saying the medical field has come very very far in diabetes management. I remember quite well the medical supplies my dad had to purchase for me at the Welch pharmacy before we got home from the hospital. First, was the injection kit that consisted of a glass syringe and plunger plus two sharp injection needles. Disposable insulin syringes and needles were nonexistent for me in 1965. The entire injection set had to be boiled for at least five minutes to destroy bacteria. Our water supply in Southern West Virginia had contaminants, so I was never quite sure about sterilization. The more I used those two needles, the duller they became. My injections hurt and often left bruising. The second purchase at the pharmacy was Tes-Tape, a light yellow paper on a spool and enclosed in a blue plastic casing. This required urine dipping with a small strip of the Tes-Tape at least four times a day. It was not as accurate or as convenient as our contemporary means of testing. I would urinate into a small paper cup and then dip the Tes-Tape in and out of it quickly. The amount of sugar in my urine was determined by the color change on the Tes-Tape strip. Dark green meant a lot of sugar in your urine. No color change meant no sugar in the urine. The third purchase my dad made was for two kinds of insulin. I had been prescribed Lente, a 24-hour long-acting insulin that was cloudy in color. Before it was injected, it had to be rolled in the palm of the hand carefully as to mix well and not create bubbles. The second insulin was Semi-Lente, a clear insulin that worked much more quickly. The two insulins could be drawn into the one syringe simultaneously though generally not recommended. But, with a very dull needle point, would you have wanted to inject yourself twice? I never did!

Here is one more amazing fact! For both bottles of insulin, Dad paid less than ten dollars. The required bottle of alcohol and cotton balls were less than a dollar each. Disposable needle points were made available about a year or two later. They were a big advantage even though the glass insulin syringe and plunger still required boiling in water. I was in my first year of college before the entire disposable insulin syringe became available. That was convenient since boiling was no longer necessary. Hemoglobin A1C's were nonexistent in the 1960's. My doctor required me to keep a written record of Tes-Tape readings. A blood glucose test was almost always done during each visit to the doctor. It helped the doctor to determine if any insulin dosage adjustments were necessary. I never really minded having blood drawn out of the best vein in my arm. Blood glucose testing was usually done every three or four months. This best vein collapsed after about ten years.

Chapter 3

High School Years as a Diabetic, 1965-1967

What I remember most about grades eleven and twelve was getting adapted to a whole new way of life. Medical requirements, already described in the last chapter, were now a daily part of my life. The grim reality was I would die if I ate just anything I wanted or quit taking insulin. There was another life- threatening danger that always loomed over me. This was low-blood sugar, and I was warned it could kill me. Actually, my blood sugar would test high most of the time throughout high school. However, marching in the high school band brought new challenges. I remember the very first time I experienced an insulin reaction or hypoglycemia. Our high school band was marching in the Veteran's Day Parade, and the parade route was about a mile long. I always played the first trumpet part because it was usually the melody. I used a lot of additional energy to play very loud and full because we had only three trumpets. The second and third trumpet players played harmony parts. It was my firm belief I kept the band together because I was the loudest performer. Therefore, I always tried very hard to do better than my best. I hadn't known what to expect from an insulin reaction or low blood sugar. I remember soaking my black, white and gold band uniform inside and out with sweat. My head sweated so much that I had a terrible time keeping on my hat, even with a chinstrap. I didn't fully understand why this was happening because I had eaten a snack on the school bus before parade lineup. I just kept playing my trumpet and marching as if nothing was wrong. That was a big mistake! I lost track of who I was and why I was playing a trumpet in a parade. My lips tingled and felt numb. Just as suddenly as all this took place, I remembered I had placed some candy in my side uniform pocket. I yelled at the second trumpet player to play my part. I stopped playing and ate the candy quickly. Minutes later, I barely had enough energy to finish marching or to even play my instrument. There would be many many more life instances of low blood sugars *(also called insulin reactions or hypoglycemia)* that would not turn out as well.

Chapter 4

First Year of College as a Diabetic, 1967-1968

I graduated from Iaeger High School at the age of seventeen in June of 1967. I had been a member of the National Honor Society and was academically in the top ten percent of my graduating class. I was college-bound and was accepted at Marshall University in Huntington, WV. As a music trumpet major, I was expected to join the Marshall University Band. I did with much enthusiasm. I had sort of learned how to avoid insulin reactions during our two-hour marching band practices. I usually ate a candy bar before practice knowing that a meal would be waiting for me at the University Dining Hall afterwards. My first insulin reaction at Marshall University came after one of these practices. Band practice had just ended, and I was sweating profusely. I was holding my trumpet and could not remember where I had left my case. I was mentally confused and too embarrassed to ask for help. I began to feel very strange. I saw very weird and twisted geometric designs in blinding colors in my mind. I was trying to determine what I should do. I knew I had to walk a short distance to the University Dining Hall before it closed. Even though this had been my normal routine, I had to think real hard where the Dining Hall was even located. I felt like I was literally floating in the air while walking.

That wasn't all that happened. A precious student started talking to me, but I couldn't respond. My brain just could not comprehend what she said. She took me by the hand and led me to the dining hall. She even made sure I got my tray of food. I never saw her again. Could she have been an angel sent by God?

These were very strange experiences during my early history of low blood sugars. There were times when I didn't realize I was experiencing a low blood sugar. This was especially troublesome. Sometimes it would happen during an exam of some kind. My mind would just go completely blank.

I found that majoring in music on a university campus soon became strenuous and very demanding because of the high-performance standards. I was not only involved in marching band and its numerous trips to away football games, but I also sang in the Marshall University Concert Choir. Each week, I took an hour lesson on trumpet because it was my major, and a thirty-minute lesson on piano because it was my minor. The minimum practice required for trumpet majors was ten hours per week and for piano minors, five hours per week. I spent exhausting hours in the practice rooms. Many times I did not feel well enough to practice, but I forced myself anyway. I discovered that when I was tired, I couldn't focus well on my weekly performance assignments. I managed an A- on piano and a C+ on trumpet. The trumpet was just too much for me to physically handle, so I dropped it as my major second semester. I then elected Piano as a major and Voice as a minor.

My diabetes, in the meantime, was largely neglected. I took my daily shots of insulin and tried to watch what I ate. I definitely went more liberal on carbohydrates like chips, popcorn, and ice cream and rarely had time to do my urine testing. I suspect my blood sugar was much higher than it should have been.

But after all, I wasn't accountable to any doctor during my first year of college, and I was constantly busy and on the move. In my thinking, this would surely balance out my eating habits with my blood sugar levels. In spite of gaining ten pounds, I wasn't concerned about my diabetes in the least.

Chapter 5

An Amazing Spiritual Transformation,

September 22, 1967

Grandmother Spitzer, my maternal grandmother, was the first one to talk to me about accepting Jesus Christ as my personal Savior. She shared with me how she had become a Christian at the age of seventeen in a Methodist church. She explained how important it was for me to allow Jesus Christ to come into my heart. I must have been about seven years of age. She also told me that God had given her a vision of me before I was born. Her vision was that one day I would be playing piano in church and blessing many people.

At the age of thirteen, I was devoutly religious. Grand-dad Spitzer was a church deacon, and he had regularly taken me to the Baptist church he attended.

On occasion, he had talked to me about *being born again*. I didn't fully understand what *being born again* involved. I just dismissed it from my thinking.

At the age of thirteen, I was asked to regularly play the piano for church services.

Grand-dad Spitzer made sure I also attended Sunday school. Maude Whistler, a precious sweet Christian, wanted to train me for the music ministry of the church. She was a public school teacher and taught at the middle school I had attended.

I had just become an overzealous member of a Girls' Leadership Society. I was motivated to play the piano because doing so gave me an excellent opportunity to earn a service badge for this Leadership Society. In reality, I had already made this Girls' Leadership meeting place my church, and the Supreme Leader of the Universe my deity. By the time I was seventeen, I believed I was God's gift to humanity. I had obtained the highest leadership medallion and had enough leadership badges to choke an elephant. If anyone was going to Heaven, it would be me. God's *Grand Scale in the Sky* would allow me in. Already, I had become the top leader of my local society and district society. I had also held two leadership offices in the West Virginia State Girls' Leadership Society. I was proud to have been respected for my high leadership ranking within this society.

The church served me a purpose, so I attended faithfully. But, the Holy Spirit made sure I heard the Gospel again and again in that little Baptist church. Little did I know that God was preparing me to become a lifelong minister of music in the local church. I was seventeen years old when I graduated from Iaeger High School in June of 1967.

I began preparing for college at Marshall University. As a yearly event, my family always traveled to visit relatives in South Carolina and in Florida during the summer months. After visiting two maternal uncles in South Carolina, we arrived at my Aunt Pat's home in Cocoa, Florida. Aunt Pat was mom's baby sister, and she was a born-again Christian who dearly loved the Lord Jesus Christ. There never was any doubt in my mind how much she prayed for me.

Some of the family and I attended Aunt Pat's church that Sunday. It was Merritt Island Baptist Church and Adrian Rogers was pastor. As I heard Adrian Rogers preach, the Holy Spirit brought me under deep conviction. He preached a message that made me realize how much I needed to accept Jesus Christ as my personal Lord and Savior. There wasn't any *Grand Scale in the Sky* that measured your good deeds against your bad to see if you entered Heaven or not. I was lost and bound for Hell and knew it beyond any doubt. I was scared and sat frozen in the pew as Adrian Rogers preached. I think Aunt Pat must have noticed because she questioned me about it later. The Holy Spirit was indeed preparing me to make the most important decision in my life regarding my eternal destiny.

I entered Marshall University, in Huntington, WV, in the fall of 1967. My piano professor was Eugenia McMullen, a graduate of Cincinnati Conservatory Of Music. I could have studied piano under any one of several different piano professors there, but my wonderful Lord Jesus made sure it would be Eugenia McMullen. Aunt Pat must have really been praying for my salvation, because this all happened shortly after I had visited her church in Merritt Island, Florida. In her piano studio, immediately after my first piano lesson, Eugenia asked me if I had ever been born-again. I was really shocked that she could ask me such a question. To me, it seemed so inappropriate and unprofessional of her. I responded to her question in the negative. She invited me to attend her church which was Grace Gospel Church in Huntington, WV. There was to be a missionary conference, and I accepted her invitation. She and her husband, Don, drove out to the Marshall campus to take me to their church that Friday night.

Rachel Saint, wife of one of the missionaries martyred by the Auca Indian Tribe of South America, spoke that night. The story she shared later became the basis of the motion picture called *End of the Spear.*

As the McMullens and I were about to leave the church, Bill Holly, the Assistant Pastor, stopped me and asked me if I had ever been born-again.

I said no. He then asked me if I would like to be born-again, and I said yes.

I followed him into his church office, and he led me through God's plan of salvation verse by verse from the Bible. I was gloriously saved! My burden of sin and self-righteous were rolled away, and I was set free. Hallelujah, the *miracle of being born-again* had just happened. Even to this very moment, at age sixty-nine, I know that if were to die, Heaven will be my eternal home. There is no sickness in Heaven, so good-by to diabetes. Praise the Lord!

I was so excited about my Lord Jesus Christ after I got saved. I felt I had to tell the world what had just happened, and I really tried to. Grace Gospel Church had a large Christian tract ministry. My favorite tract was a red one called *The Little Bible*. I liked it because it had God's plan of salvation verse by verse. I would keep a supply on hand by frequently taking a few off of the Church's tract rack to give to others on and off campus.

My desire, as a newly born-again Christian, was to serve my Lord Jesus Christ through the musical gifts He had given to me. I had worked hard to develop these gifts while growing up, so I wanted to use them for God's Glory.

As a girl who loved to sing, I sang and shared my testimony in church after church.

Eugenia and Don McMullen became my closest Christian friends for life.

She hinted to me, not long after I was saved, that perhaps I should leave Marshall University and transfer to a Christian University. It was probably one of the most conservative Christian universities in the nation. Her son, Jim, was in this Christian School's high school, so they invited me to visit the campus and to view a grand opera that the university's music department was performing. I had been studying voice under the former New York Metropolitan Opera Singer, Jane Hobson Shepherd. I had learned so much and wanted to remain her student.

She had a big and powerful voice and so did I. I should have remained with her. Many years later, I deeply regretted not doing so.

This Christian University definitely attracted my interests, so in the fall of 1968, I transferred there.

Chapter 6

A Christian University, 1968-1972

I arrived on the campus of this university in August of 1968. Just two weeks before, I had been rushed by ambulance to Grace Hospital in Welch, WV because mom could not wake me up from a nap. We both had been shopping that day and had done lots of walking. After we got home, my blood sugar dropped without me realizing it. I was exhausted and decided to nap before supper. I didn't wake up until moved into a private room at the hospital. Mom was frantic and worried about me continuing college at a Christian University. In fact, she did not like the idea at all. Several times she had tried to talk me out of it. I simply told her that I had but one life to live, and I wanted to live it for the Lord Jesus Christ. I now see what she was trying to help me understand.

Not too many weeks after I arrived at this Christian University, I was found unconscious by the supervisor of my dormitory. My schedule of classes required more walking than I had been used to. I had decided to nap before eating at the campus Dining Common at 6:00 PM. The University required every student on campus to attend the evening meal. When I didn't show up at my assigned table, I was reported and checked on immediately. It was probably best because I could have easily died from a severe insulin reaction.

The strict rules at this University never truly bothered me. My first year there went well. It seemed an ideal environment for a Christian student to be, and everyone professed to be a Christian. I had decided to continue my major in music education with a proficiency in voice. The Voice Teacher I was assigned to was nothing like the opera singer who had taught me at Marshall University.

As her student, instead of encouraging me, she made feel like a complete failure during every lesson. This voice teacher at the Christian University told me that my loud, strong voice would only insult people when I sang. I couldn't believe it, this was the vocal gift that God had given me. My sole purpose for mastering singing technique was to communicate the gospel more effectively.

Jane Hobson Shepherd had taught me to sing traditional art songs and German Lieder very well and dramatically with my big voice. Now, I was being told to sing *mousy* and to make *little to no movement* when I sang. This left little room for me to sing straight from the depth of my soul. I just couldn't imagine myself standing like *The Statue of Liberty in New York Harbor* every time I sang. I really made an effort to meet their *one-way, their way, method for singing*, but I failed their Sophomore Voice Proficiency Platform. A panel of five of their voice faculty told me I had no ability to sing because my voice had been improperly trained by my former teacher at Marshall University.

I had also taken a music theory semester exam during one of my insulin reactions. I just sat in my chair sweating and afraid of getting into trouble if I ate candy in class. I was so devastated through failing my Voice Platform Exam, that I didn't do well on any of my semester music exams. I didn't pursue piano as a major either. I felt a deep fear that failure would happen to me again. I felt the Christian University Music Department had *flushed me down the toilet.*

They decided I had no singing talent, and I became suicidal. I became very bitter in the many years that followed. I almost left music entirely. However, I remained at the university and graduated in 1972 with a Bachelor of Science degree in Secondary Education. God had a marvelous plan for me in Church Music Ministry and in Music Education. It was yet to become realized.

Bitterness slowly became a stronghold in my young Christian life. Even though I continued playing piano, I found myself saying and doing things that I knew were not right. I became enslaved to bitterness, and it was an unpleasant taskmaster. *Never allow yourself to fall into any trap of bitterness because it is straight from Hell. It allows Satan to rob a Christian of their internal peace and joy that comes from being a child of God.* Almighty God delivered me from bitterness in 1984. As a result, I wrote a personal letter to each of the five voice faculty members and asked for their forgiveness for holding bitterness towards them. After this happened, God began to bless me with multiple gifts in music and other creative talents. I gloriously experienced the overflowing power of God's Holy Spirit again and again in Christian service.

I married Paul Worley, a now retired Chief Petty Officer in the U.S. Coast Guard, on November 21, 1973. Paul was a Third Class Petty Officer in the U.S. Coast Guard, and I was actively teaching social studies in one of Corpus Christi's Christian schools at the time of our marriage.

The McMullen's had moved to Edinburg, Texas. She was a Professor of Piano at Pan American University. Before I married Paul, I drove to her house weekly to take private voice lessons at Pan American University. I was thrilled to sing Franz Schubert's German lieder again. My voice professor taught me much like Jane Hobson Shepherd had done. He encouraged me much. My dramatic soprano voice slowly began to return, but I rarely sang in public for fear it would suddenly sound mousy and weak with bad vibrato. I discontinued the voice lessons soon after my marriage to Paul.

I had to drive very carefully every time I visited the McMullen family in the Rio Grande Valley. My blood sugars would fluctuate. I would fall asleep momentarily while driving or do additional dangerous driving. One time, I caught myself driving eighty miles per hour on the wrong side of a two-lane highway. I found a little country store and purchased a candy bar to eat. But, after my blood sugar came up, I felt totally wiped out. This was no way to be driving, and I knew it. But, my next voice lesson had top priority, and I would continue my risky journey down Highway 77 to the McMullen's home in Edinburg, Texas.

I serve a wonderful Lord, and He must have used an army of angels to watch over me. I ended up unconscious one time in an insulin reaction at my Christian school. After someone finally got me awake, I drank orange juice and recovered. My energy had completely left. But, I never allowed a *low blood- sugar wipe-out* to deter me from going right back to what I had been doing.

Paul proposed to me on the campus of Pan American University. Eugenia played piano for our wedding and her son Jim ushered. Don took our wedding pictures without charge. It was a wonderful event. Paul had to learn real fast what to do in case I had a low blood sugar. He handled it very well. Paul has saved my life many times over the years. We were to be parents of two sons and one adopted daughter. I did have children in spite of what the doctor had predicted after the onset of my diabetes in 1965. I also have lived more than twenty-five years. In fact, this year of 2019 marks my fifty-fourth year of living with Diabetes Mellitus. Thank you Lord Jesus!

Chapter 7

Mobile, Alabama, 1975-1980

The year was 1975. Paul had gotten his orders for U.S. Coast Guard Aviation Training Center in Mobile, Alabama. On September 11, 1976, I gave birth to our first son. Stephen was born three weeks early at seven pounds and twelve ounces. Other than a brief period of bilirubin, he was a very healthy baby. I had no real problems with my diabetes during or after this pregnancy.

I did experience difficulties with my diabetes before the birth of my second son born twenty-two months later. I experienced a low blood sugar that rendered me unconscious late in this pregnancy. Fortunately, Paul and a friend were able to get me awake. My nineteen-month-old Stephen was all right even though left alone for a few hours. When Paul and his friend arrived, Stephen was seated on the floor with a super-soaked cloth diaper and eating cereal out of a box.

On July 22, 1978, I gave birth to our second son. Philip was born five weeks early at six pounds and three ounces. Thanks to the help of the Mobile, Alabama LaLeche League, I was able to nurse Philip until he was almost four years old.

In Mobile, I played piano and sang solos in different churches. I'll never forget Westwood Baptist Church. I was playing organ there one

Sunday after Philip had been born. I reached across the organ to set the stops on their Hammond Organ. My breast milk dropped unexpectedly and wet the entire front of my dress. Another time, I was standing behind the pulpit preparing to sing a solo. My mind drew a blank, and I was sweating a lot. Apologizing, I excused myself and moved quickly to the nursery. I was able to eat some of their cookies.

Breast-feeding Philip actually helped my diabetes. It enabled me to take less insulin and to stabilize my *brittle diabetes* much better. He slept in the bed with Paul and me for about the first three months. He never had colic or needed to be burped as long as I didn't eat any food that would create gas. At times, he would nurse me without even waking me up. There was no formula routine!

We lived in Mobile, Alabama until 1980. We met some truly wonderful people. I prayed that one day we would be able to move back into the house we had bought. Philip was two and Stephen was almost four when we made our next move across the Pacific Ocean to the Hawaiian Islands.

Stephen almost died from epiglottitis four months before our move. There had been eight children with epiglottis in Mobile that year. Stephen was the only child who lived. Stephen today is forty-three and works as a trouble-shooter for Apple Computer. He also has an Acoustical Engineering Degree from Texas State University, San Marcos, Texas. Philip is forty-one and has a B.A. Degree in Ministry from Stark College and Seminary, Corpus Christi, Texas.

Chapter 8

Barber's Point, Hawaii, 1980-1983

We arrived in Honolulu, Hawaii in August, 1980. My blood-sugar level was the best it had ever been. Paul was stationed at the U.S. Coast Guard Air Station, Barber's Point, Hawaii. Because of Stephens' allergies and my diabetes, we were fortunate to obtain base housing at the Barber's Point Navy Base. I was appointed to a good Navy doctor of internal medicine. All my diabetic supplies, visits to the doctor, and prescriptions were provided free.

Hawaii was a beautiful place, and a melting pot of all cultures and languages. I soon became organist of a local Baptist Church in Ewa Beach. The churches' congregation were warm friendly people who welcomed my family and I into the church with open arms. I sang in their choir, sang solos, and taught the adult Sunday school a time or two. I particularly loved their monthly Sunday Night Fellowship Dinners. Their traditional native Hawaiian prepared meals were scrumptious. It was the very first time I had ever eaten mangoes, papayas, and pineapples picked fresh that morning. The cakes they made and the meats they prepared were excellent. Usually, I would have to take a little more insulin to cover what I ate. I don't recommend this because usually I took too much insulin, causing my blood sugar to drop too low. I would then raise it back up with sweets or juice. I would repeat this process over and over, causing my blood sugar and insulin intake to yo yo wildly. *Never inject more insulin so you can indulge in sweets or more carbohydrates.* It can be fatal, and can cause weight gain over a short period of time.

In Hawaii, I took a very active part in the Suzuki Violin Association of Hawaii. Stephen began his violin lessons at age four and Philip at age three. I followed the Suzuki method thoroughly and both sons did very well. The two boys played solos for Suzuki Concerts on the islands of Oahu and Maui. I was one of the Suzuki Association's several piano accompanists for concerts. I did this in exchange for violin lessons. Philip and another three-year-old student named Robin, played Bach's *Minuet 1* as a duet with the Maui Symphony. Stephen, on the other hand, was a star Suzuki Student. He played solos in nearly every concert and won first place in a State of Hawaii Strings Competition. By the age of five, he had advanced to book four of the Suzuki classical repertoire.

It nearly broke my heart when we had to leave Hawaii in 1983. God did two great things for me as a result of my experience in Hawaii. First, the Suzuki experience brought me back into the realization I could indeed become a music educator. This dream had been destroyed at the Christian university. I had more to give as an instrumentalist than as a vocalist in music education.

Secondly, I received my first insulin pump from Tripler A.M.C. *(Army Medical Center)* on the island of Oahu. I was one of the first two hundred Americans to receive an insulin pump. To me, it was an amazing instrument, second only to the invention of the wheel. It was almost the size of the smallest *Kindle Fire 7*. Also, I was taught a way to actually measure my blood glucose level for the first time. This was incredible! The medical staff at Tripler A.M.C. tested me six times to see if I could properly read the results of this fingerstick. If I failed, I couldn't receive the pump. There wasn't any glucometer at this time. I had to read a strip similar to a Tes-Tape strip. I learned the meanings of two new words in diabetes management. One word was bolus, and the other word was basal. I thought the bolus was really cool. Any time my blood sugar tested too high, I would pump a bolus amount of insulin to bring it back to normal. The ratio was determined by my Tripler A.M.C. doctor. The basal rate would pump a small amount of insulin every hour to keep me stable. I was very proud of my pump!

Chapter 9

Elizabeth City, North Carolina, 1983-1990

Right after receiving my insulin pump from Tripler A.M.C., Paul got orders to teach in the Coast Guard Aviation Technical Training Center in Elizabeth City, NC. We moved there in the summer of 1983. I would surely miss my involvement with the Suzuki Association of Hawaii.

Fortunately for me, I was able to locate a doctor to regulate my insulin pump. He was located in Virginia Beach, VA, about fifty miles north of Elizabeth City, NC. The only real disadvantage was the driving distance and having to call long distance. My blood sugars didn't do as well as I had expected. I gained too much weight on the pump. The doctor in Virginia Beach took me off of the insulin pump in 1989. This really upset me! I tried not to think about it too much. Paul had a transfer coming up, and this had created much stress.

Our two sons and I had continued our violin lessons at the College of the Albemarle in Elizabeth City. It wasn't like it had been before in Hawaii. Stephen, at age 10, performed a full-scale violin concert at the home of an Elizabeth City physician. I chose to continue my Suzuki Violin Training at East Carolina University in Greeneville, NC. I completed training for books one and two. After this, I founded the *Suzuki Players of the Albemarle* for students who wanted to learn Suzuki Piano or Suzuki

Violin. We were stationed in Elizabeth City, NC for seven years, and I had a significant number of students. This gave me opportunity to be the music educator I dreamed of becoming. I took the North Carolina Teacher's exam to become a public school music teacher and passed it.

The only problem was we were not in North Carolina long enough for me to use it. I did substitute for an elementary music specialist in Elizabeth City. I really admired this young talented lady, and she really liked the work that I did for her.

As far as music ministry went, I was in six different churches. My favorite was the Protestant chapel on the Coast Guard Base. The Chaplain was a Baptist, so I became very comfortable playing the piano there. Military base chapels have unique ministries because of the many Protestant denominations represented.

Philip, my youngest son, was soon to be five-years-old after we moved to Elizabeth City. He was having some medical issues that had already been checked out in Hawaii. One issue was his erratic behavior that would cause him to grimace and become bug-eyed several times during the day. There were other manifestations that I won't go into. In addition, Philip always walked with a slight limp. There wasn't any doctor he had seen who could offer a clear diagnosis.

Finally, he was diagnosed through the Department of Public Health in Elizabeth City. He had mild cerebral palsy and at least two epileptic seizure disorders. His unusual behavior was a form of epilepsy.

I always wondered if my diabetes could have contributed to his diagnosis.

Only the good Lord knows. At three, his violin performance was extraordinary.

Chapter 10

Our Sweet Little Baby from Seoul, Korea

Paul was still stationed in Elizabeth City, NC in 1987. We had heard that the Principal and his wife of the Christian school our boys attended had just adopted a South Korean baby girl. Paul and I had always secretly hoped for a little girl to complete our family of four. After praying about adoption, we began our adoption journey in the office of a social worker in Pasquotank County, NC. Elizabeth City was the county seat. We were approved by the social worker and the adoption was finalized. Our next question was how soon would we have our baby girl?

The South Korean adoption agency sent us a letter stating that unless I could obtain medical clearance because of my insulin pump, we could not adopt. They also had strict weight guidelines. If you were obese, forget adoption!Somehow, they had a misunderstanding about my insulin pump. They believed I was attached to a large machine of some kind that pumped insulin into me all the time. They thought I was non ambulatory and could not possibly care for an infant. The doctor that handled my diabetes cleared up this misunderstanding. Paul and I finally were approved by the South Korean government. The next letter we received from South Korea stated our nine-month-old infant girl would be arriving with escort at the Washington DC National Airport on October 19, 1988. We were thrilled!

God also gave us an unexpected confirmation just days before we received our approval letter from South Korea. The hostess of the *700 Club* in Virginia Beach, Virginia, stated the following during their prayer time:

"The Lord has shown to me that there is a couple who have been waiting on the completion of an adoption. You have encountered an unexpected delay based upon the wife's medical condition. You will be hearing soon from the country of the infant's origin. The Lord wants me to tell you that this baby girl will soon become a part of your family."

I claimed this confirmation. Three days later Paul and I received the news that our baby girl was on her way.

We left Elizabeth City in the summer of 1990. Paul had received orders to the U.S. Coast Guard Air Station, Miami, Florida. We thought it best to keep our family close to my Aunt Pat in Cocoa, Florida. Nothing significant happened with my diabetes. We were in Cocoa for only one year. I was privileged to perform in the Merritt Island Baptist Church Orchestra as a violinist. I also taught in the church's School of Fine Arts for a short period of time.

Having a B.S. degree in Secondary Education from a nonaccredited Christian University was greatly to my disadvantage. The university always assured its education majors that there would be plenty of positions available for them in public schools. All we had to do was take the state teacher certification test.

I scored the lowest score of all the education graduating seniors at this Christian University because I was in an insulin reaction throughout most the test. We were told not to get up or to eat anything during the testing. I was afraid to do either. I could hardly read the words in the test booklet because of blurred vision. I couldn't have told anyone my name, let alone answer the test questions. I should have let someone know.

The Christian University I graduated from feared their high academic and Christian standards would be compromised if they accepted state certification.

Liberty University in Lynchberg, Virginia was willing to help me and many other graduates of this university. Liberty University is a great Christian school with full state accreditation. I followed through with their academic plan and was able to receive my teacher certification in music education from the state of Alabama.

In the summer of 1991, Paul was transferred a second time to the U.S. Coast Guard Aviation Training Center in Mobile, Alabama.

Chapter 11

Back to Mobile, Alabama

I was so excited about getting back to Mobile, Alabama in the summer of 1991, that I actually kissed the ground at the Alabama welcome station. We had left Alabama on a transfer to Hawaii in 1980. Both of my boys had been born in Mobile, and we still owned the house we had purchased a few months before Stephen was born. In my mind, everything in Mobile would be just the way we left it. I thought that this would be our last military move since Paul would be retiring soon. Surely, God was directing us back to Mobile, Alabama. I expected a teaching position in public school after Paul retired.

Sadly, Mobile was not the same. The Alabama public school system was not filling elementary school music teacher positions once they were vacated by the music teacher's retirement. I had already taken the Alabama State Music Teachers' exam and passed it. No one in the colleges and universities in Mobile gave me any word of encouragement about obtaining a music specialist position in an elementary school. I was really discouraged. In November of 1991, I had my first heart attack. The bad news about a very possible failure to become an elementary music specialist in Mobile or surrounding area could have caused me to have this heart attack.

I wanted job security after Paul retired. I enrolled in a Medical Assistant Training Program in Mobile. I completed training for both medical assistant and medical transcriptionist successfully. I did one internship in Mobile, Alabama and the other internship in Corpus Christi, Texas.

I had opportunity to play violin and baritone horn in the church orchestra of Cottage Hill Baptist Church, one of the largest Baptist churches in Alabama. I am so thankful for all the wonderful people I met there. They prayed for me every time I had a crisis with my blood sugar. They graciously prayed for any need my family had.

Paul and I both knew that Mobile was not going to be the city we would live in after his retirement. Everything seemed very different. The people in the neighborhood where we had lived before were not quite as friendly. I think some of them ignored us because we had a Korean daughter. I always had an unsettled feeling that something bad could erupt with our neighbors. I was greatly relieved when we left Mobile, Alabama in the summer of 1992. I had to leave ahead of my family because I was to begin my medical transcription internship at Bay Area Hospital, Corpus Christi.

Just a few months before actual retirement, Paul got orders to the U.S. Coast Guard Air Station in Corpus Christi, TX. This was a blessing! Paul was back home in the town he grew up. It would be great to have relatives living in the same town. This had occurred only briefly before in Cocoa, Florida.

Chapter 12

Home Sweet Home in Corpus Christi, Texas

Corpus Christi, Texas has been called the *Sparkling City by the Sea*. I was looking forward to settling in one place for the first time since Paul and I married in 1973. It can be difficult on a family to settle in and then suddenly receive military orders. Our boys were old enough to regret losing friends and leaving their schools. Paul and I regretted losing great friends also. In my *heart of hearts*, I knew Corpus Christi, Texas was the place God wanted us to be.

While living in Cocoa, Florida, I had been without close supervision of my type 1 diabetes. I only got to see an Air Force doctor two times at the Patrick Air Force Base in Cocoa Beach, Florida. Seeing a military doctor is not ideal for an insulin-dependent diabetic, because about the time a doctor really gets to know you and your diabetes, he or she gets a military transfer.

I was also back in Mobile, Alabama for a year, so it wasn't enough time for my doctor there to get a close look at my diabetes. When my first heart attack happened, I was living in Mobile. I had a close brush with death because the Valium that was given to me during my first heart cauterization nearly killed me. I actually had a very pleasant after-death experience, but my Lord Jesus brought me back. I felt that God was not through with me yet because a great work still lay ahead for me to do. It would not be in the medical field. The heart specialist and the doctor of internal medicine I had at Providence Hospital in Mobile were very good. I wasn't under their medical care long enough to really matter. My family and I had moved back to Corpus Christi, Texas by July of 1991.

After completing my internship as a medical transcriptionist at Bay Area Hospital, I tried doing transcription for a Neurology Clinic. Lacking real experience, I was no match for the two medical transcriptionists already working there. I just could not do the transcription fast enough. I then worked as a front office certified medical assistant for a Nephrology Office. I did filing and records.

At last, I got a job from an insurance company drawing blood and testing urine.

This job was okay, but I had to drive all over South Texas and in the Rio Grande Valley. My type 1 diabetes again became a safety issue. I did this job for about four months. Being in the medical field was not what I was meant to do, and I knew it. My mother, in WV, had developed cancer in one of her kidneys, so this validated my reason for quitting the insurance company. I went to WV to be with mom and to drive her to medical appointments.

Chapter 13

Would My Diabetes Allow Me to Teach?

My hope began to sparkle as I prepared to take the Texas state exams for a professional certification to teach and a certification to become a public school music specialist. A physician in Corpus Christi told me I would not last a year in the music classroom. But, I was determined to obtain the career of my dreams. I would not allow my diabetes to stand in my way. The year of 1993 would be a momentous year because good news was on its way!

After returning from taking care of my mother in WV, I got a telephone call from the Corpus Christi I.S.D. *(Independent School District)* Music Office. The Music Department Head offered me a permanent music substitute position for Corpus Christi I.S.D. I would be assigned to the new Luther Jones Elementary School and to Club Estates Elementary School. No words could possibly describe how happy and fulfilled I felt. Earlier in 1993, I had substituted for the three elementary music teachers at the Chula Vista Academy of Fine Arts. All three had been very impressed with my work and had recommended me to the Music Department Head of the Corpus Christi I.S.D. This was a lifetime dream realized! I took the two Texas certification examinations in September and passed.

During my first month in the public school music classroom, I had several low blood sugar episodes. I was a very physically active music teacher. I choose to move around a lot, especially with kindergarten through second grade. Besides that, I had to push a music cart loaded with instruments, music records, and music books at Club Estates Elementary School. Once, while teaching third grade classes there, I was doing the singing and movements to *The Long-legged Sailor.*

Suddenly and unexpectedly, the sweat started pouring off of me. I had candy aboard my cart, but I wondered if I should eat it in front of the children. I postponed this action and barely made it until the end of class. After class, I pushed my cart out of the classroom after unplugging and reloading it. I could have passed out any moment. After I knew the coast was clear, I grabbed four or five *Bits of Honey* candy and ate these quickly. I pushed my cart into the next third grade classroom assuming my low blood sugar problem had been satisfactorily solved. It wasn't! This class was the one I visited right before lunch.

I had no sooner unloaded the music books off my cart and distributed some instruments than the sweat started pouring off me once again. *I had to use what little presence of mind I had and decide carefully what to do without the children being alarmed.* Carefully I pushed the music cart to the nearest outlet to plug in the record player. I hid myself behind the record player and ate some huge orange slice gumdrops as quickly as I could. Naturally, my lips were tingling and my hair was completely wet because of the low blood sugar. But, I still managed to complete my lesson plans for this class. I had lunch and completed my teaching for the day. I told absolutely no one at Club Estates Elementary about this low blood sugar crisis. I wasn't willing to run the risk of not being hired as a full-time Elementary Music Teacher for the Corpus Christi I.S.D.

My other serious low-blood sugar episode occurred not long afterwards at Jones Elementary School. It was on a day I taught first grade and kindergarten.

Any music specialist knows you do not sit down at all when you are teaching these two grade levels. They require constant movement and a change of activity about every five to eight minutes. I was leading them along and suddenly I realized I was in trouble. It was my last class of the day, and after doing the same routine for six classes, I suddenly realized I had not eaten enough for lunch. I had been concerned about my weight and had eaten only a salad and a fruit for lunch.

That was a huge mistake because I did not have enough carbohydrates to cover all the activities. I had no candy or emergency juices to bring up my blood sugar level. I knew I wasn't in any condition to march, clap, chant, jump, hop, or pretend I was the big baboon at the animal fair combing my auburn hair. So, I gathered all the children and had them sit in front of the piano. I played the piano while they sang their favorite nursery rhyme songs. The best behaved child got to accompany with a drum. It amazed me at how fast my Lord Jesus had given me this idea. After the children had left with their teacher, my blood sugar had dropped so low, I couldn't have told you my name. I was so mentally confused, I had to ask someone how to get to the school office. The school nurse came to my rescue. I honestly don't know if this got reported or not. This happened on a Friday, and I would be back at Club Estates on Monday. I did two week rotations between the two schools. I didn't hear from the Corpus Christi I.S.D. Music Department Head or from either Principal, and I was glad!

During the first Friday of October of 1993, I received a telephone call from a close-by neighboring school district just ten miles from Corpus Christi. I was called in for an interview for a full-time music teaching position at their intermediate school for grades four, five, and six. To this day, I haven't a clue as to how they knew about me. I was accepted at their interview and began my full-time teaching there on October 12, 1993.

Chapter 14

My First Seven Years of Teaching

On the morning of October 12, 1993, I walked into this school district's intermediate school not knowing what to expect. I had candy in my blazer pocket in case I developed low blood sugar. I had over forty fifth graders enter my classroom. They didn't know what to expect and neither did I. As a first year teacher, I will never forget that first day and this first period class. Obviously, this class was badly overcrowded. I had to limit my planned routine of activities. There simply was not enough room. Two groups of boys almost started a gang war over an argument of where to sit. The talkers would not stop talking until I started writing discipline slips. I couldn't write them fast enough, and I think they knew it. I was then unfair! All the strategies I thought I knew on how to manage a class *went up in smoke!* The intermediate school was an excellent boot camp for this beginning music teacher. My seven years of experience in this school provided me valuable training in teaching strategies, spontaneous creativity, directing a choir, and classroom management.

I decided to arrange the chairs in a circle around the room instead of in four straight rows. I was an activities-oriented music teacher, not a music theory teacher. I also tried very hard to put the students in a boy-girl assigned seating order. As long as you can keep talkers and trouble-makers separated, you have half a chance as a music teacher. The problem was that there were always too many talkers and trouble-makers in nearly every class, especially grade five. Seating charts were very useful. Under advice of the Principal, I started a *Race to Recess Contest for all my classes*. The best-behaved fourth and fifth grade class earned an outside fifteen-minute recess for the six weeks. Stickers earned were placed on a huge chart after every class left the music classroom. Slowly, I believe most students realized my class really was for learning music and for having fun in an orderly fashion.

Teaching kept me very busy. Over time, I was able to make two combined fourth grade classes into a performing Recorder Flute Ensemble. We toured Corpus Christi and the surrounding areas at Christmas time. I think the students enjoyed doing this. I was very proud of them. My blood sugars usually were good because of all the activity I did in the music classroom. Once or twice every six weeks, I usually hit a low. I kept a small refrigerator in my classroom loaded with juices and diet drinks.

My talents began to explode early in my teaching career. I give God all the glory. I became a published composer of music for choir and recorder flute. My choral selection for Intermediate School Choir was entitled *The Ballad of the Texas Bluebonnet*. It was published in 1997, and debuted by the 100-voice *Woodrow Wilson Fifth Grade Choir* of Denton, Texas. My other music published that year was an instrumental method book entitled *Critter Classics for Recorder Flute*. With this method book, I was able to teach over a thousand students on how to play recorder flute. I later developed the book to cover all sizes of recorder flutes. In each song, I created an impressionistic sound image of an animal or insect. I believe the Fourth Grade Flour Bluff Recorder Ensemble enjoyed debuting these songs. They were very self-motivated students. I enjoyed creating the piano accompaniments too because they were strictly impressionistic. My Lord Jesus gave me unbelievable wisdom to create this music and much more as time moved along.

"If any of you lack wisdom, let him ask of God, that giveth to all men liberally, and upbraideth not; and it shall be given him." James 1:5 (KJV)

In June of 1997, the *Corpus Christi Caller Times* honored me with *Most Valuable Teacher of the Month Award*. I wrote a short article for them about myself, and it was published in a Sunday Edition of their newspaper. I also began my Master's Degree in School Counseling at Texas A&M, Corpus Christi. I graduated with this degree in August of 1999. My seven years as a music specialist for this school district would continue until June of 2000.

Chapter 15

A Near Tragedy in 1999

I was in my sixth year of teaching music at the intermediate school. My music classroom had been moved into a much smaller outside portable classroom. This added more disruption from some of my students. My usual classroom activities were greatly limited because of this additional lack of space.

I remember taking a fifth grade class back into the school building for a water/bathroom break before they were scheduled to return to class. This was something I rarely did as a music teacher. On this particular day, tensions had run high in the classroom because of disruption from a small group of boys. These boys were issued discipline slips. The two ringleaders persisted in telling me they didn't deserve discipline slips. It happened shortly before the end of class. To calm this tense situation down, I volunteered to escort the class to the bathroom and water fountain inside the school building before their classroom teachers were to escort them back to their classrooms.

While supervising this fifth grade line in the school hallway, I stepped forward and tripped. The full impact of my weight fell on my left wrist just above my hand. Even though Diabetic Nephropathy allowed only minimal pain, my lower left arm began to swell quickly because I had crushed the wrist bone. I did not have a clue as to the seriousness of this injury. My husband Paul drove me to the school's emergency medical clinic in Corpus Christi. An X-Ray was ordered, and the doctor informed me I had crushed my wrist and that it was the worst wrist injury he had ever witnessed. I was referred to an Orthopedic Arm and Hand Specialist. After visiting this medical specialist the following day, I was admitted to the hospital for my initial surgery. The doctor informed me that my injury was so serious that more than one surgery would be required.

During a second surgery, my arm came into contact with staph infection. This was the worst possible thing that could have happened to a forty-nine-year old type 1 diabetic. It was a day surgery, and I had returned home.

The next morning I noticed that the surgery site was pale red, swollen and itching. A slightly raised infectious boil had formed on top. As the day continued, the swollen area spread and turned an angry red. The infectious boil grew larger and looked like it would burst. By afternoon, I noticed a developing fever and pain. In the early evening, I was in such extreme pain that I just sat in my rocking chair and cried. It was a pain second only to childbirth.

The next morning I called for an appointment with my doctor of internal medicine. My blood sugar was very high, and I was very sick. This doctor diagnosed the infection as a type of staphylococcus and immediately sent me to my Orthopedic Surgeon. At the Orthopedic office, it was confirmed by x-ray that the staph infection had already destroyed a portion of my wrist bone.

I was admitted to a Corpus Christi hospital with elevated blood sugar and cellulitis. The nursing staff administered a continual drip of antibiotics and the wound was washed out in a whirlpool several times a day. The Orthopedic Hand and Arm Surgeon ended up doing multiple surgeries to remove the damaged bone tissue and as much of the infection as he could. After all the surgeries, antibiotics, and whirlpool therapies, the infection still threatened me. The only solution was amputation below the elbow or hyperbaric oxygen therapy. I prayed that my insurance would cover the second alternative, and it did. My surgeon was a musician also, and I believe he knew well what an amputation would mean to me.

After forty-two hyperbaric oxygen therapy sessions, I was finally out of danger. I am very appreciative of the excellent work done by the hyperbaric nursing staff. My thanks goes out to the many Christians who prayed for me, and for the Corpus Christi Baptist pastor who anointed me with oil and prayed for my total healing.

A student informant let me know the name of the boy who tripped me and caused this near tragedy. He bragged about it as a sixth grader and yet denied it in the Assistant Principal's office as a fifth grader. Young man, I know your name, and I forgive you. I also pray for you. I left this School District in June of 2000.

Chapter 16

Teaching in the Corpus Christi I.S.D., 2000-2005

God truly blessed me with a wonderful music teaching position in the Corpus Christi I.S.D. I wanted to teach music to the primary grades as well as the upper elementary. As a music teacher for two Corpus Christi Elementary Schools, I taught all grades except for kindergarten. The music rooms were large, and I had a private office of my own with a telephone. This was a tremendous blessing for me! If I had a personal emergency, I would be able to make a telephone call.

Going back and forth between two schools on a two-week rotation sent my blood-sugar nose-diving on many occasions. I always kept a large bag of gumdrops with my teaching materials. Usually the bag was empty by the end of the week. Had I been back on an insulin pump, I could have handled my diabetes much better. I don't remember passing out, but I came very close more than once.

I had already obtained a Master's Degree in School Counseling and had begun working towards a second Master's Degree in Curriculum and Instruction from Texas A.&M., Corpus Christi. I completed this second degree in December of 2004.

During my second year of teaching music in Corpus Christi, I found a doctor of internal medicine who believed it would be a good idea to allow me back on the insulin pump. She was also a diabetic and on the insulin pump. In complete confidence, I greatly admired her. She inspired me and probably saved my life multiple times. By being back on an insulin pump, I was able to manage my diabetes much more closely. I had to carry a large glucometer with my pump to calibrate my blood sugars. This guaranteed the pump to read my blood sugars more accurately.

Even though the pump greatly reduced the episodes of hypoglycemia, I used it as a tool to consume more food and sweets in the teachers' lounge. This added extra weight and was dangerous. Please take my advice and don't do it if you are on an insulin pump!

For the 2001-2002 School Year, I taught at only one Corpus Christi elementary school. The other elementary school had been closed. I loved my job of teaching music, especially to the primary grades. My principal liked for the students to perform in musicals. So did I! I worked very hard preparing the students for their musicals. Had it not been for my insulin pump regulating my blood sugars more closely, I probably would not have been able to handle the work and stress that goes into directing a children's musical. I wrote two of the musicals we performed. Second graders performed *Why Cowboys Sing in Texas* in the spring of 2003, and fourth graders performed *Garlic Greta and the Texas Outlaws* in the spring of 2005. I wrote a second-grade level book entitled <u>Garlic Greta and the Outlaws</u>. It was published in 2005 by a New York Publisher. It was from this book I created my second musical.

Chapter 17

An Unexpected Health Crisis in May of 2005

In May of 2005, I faced another life threatening experience that happened unexpectedly. Six months prior, I had experienced short periods of discomfort in my left lower back. I did not have this checked by a doctor because I didn't think the pain was that serious. Low-grade fever and malaise came on me during the first week of May. Then on May 10, an avalanche of pain came upon me suddenly. It was so bad that I could neither stand nor sit up. This was on a Monday morning. I called the school secretary and told her I would not be at school that day. I could barely talk to her because I was in so much pain. I told her that I was physically unable to call 911. She graciously did this for me, and within fifteen minutes, I was wheeled into an ambulance at my house.

My condition was diagnosed as Urethral Obstruction. I had a blockage in my left ureter that prevented it from carrying urine from my left kidney to my bladder. This condition had nothing to do with my diabetes. It was a congenital defect. It had taken fifty-five years for a very narrow ureter to finally block my urine flow. The urine had backed up into my left kidney causing it to swell and hurt. I had sepsis and a grim prognosis. My temperature in the emergency room reached 103 degrees, and I had a heart attack. I should have died, but God had other plans for me. Many people prayed for me, and I believe their prayers were answered. I didn't teach for the remainder of that school year. Several precious teachers at my school came to visit me at the hospital. I will never forget their kindness and concern. I rested well that summer.

During the summer, I thought seriously about using my Master's Degree in School Curriculum and Instruction to become an educational diagnostician. I had taken the Texas certification exam to become an educational diagnostician and had passed it. An opportunity came up in the Alice, Texas I.S.D. I interviewed for this position and was accepted.

Chapter 18

An Educational Diagnostician for the Alice I.S.D.

On my first day as an educational diagnostician for the Alice I.S.D., I entered into a *whole new world*. I am sure that most of the staff at that office wondered why a music specialist from the Corpus Christi I.S.D. was *parading around as an educational diagnostician in their neck of the woods*. It would become a revelation about to unfold, especially for me and all my co-workers.

After about three weeks, I seriously wondered why I was even there. I praise the Lord for Annette Starr, a senior educational diagnostician who trained and prevented me from derailing more than once. I praise the Lord for all the Alice I.S.D. diagnosticians who had to put up with my ignorance and inexperience.

Oh, I must not forget to thank Debbie Richardson. The homework I gave her every night would make any one want to retire early.

Honestly now, my being an educational diagnostician for one school year was not all that bad. It was very interesting but hard work. I loved testing and evaluating students. What was very confusing and difficult for me were all the many smaller details I was required to perform. *This shoe that I wanted to try on just didn't fit and I knew it!* Simply put, God did not want me to be an educational diagnostician and I knew it! I was outside of my calling in life.

My heart yearned to be back in the music classroom.

My blood sugars were probably high most of the time while working for the Alice I.S.D. There were always carbohydrates around for me to sample. A little extra bolus here and a little extra bolus there from my insulin pump put extra weight on me. I was well over two hundred pounds by the time I transferred to the Lamar C.I.S.D. to accept a music specialist position once again.

Chapter 19

Teaching in the Lamar C.I.S.D.

It is amazing at how much regional I.S.D.s can differ one from the other. The Lamar Consolidated Independent School District in Rosenberg, Texas was, by far, the best district I taught in. I accepted a music educational specialist position at Hutchinson Elementary School in the fall of 2006. The school was in its second year of operation and had already received an exemplary rating from the state of Texas. The Principal informed me he had interviewed over forty applicants for the music position I applied for. I felt very honored. The school had a strict discipline plan for the students which was enforced. The various departments and the administration congruently worked together. These attributes are important parts to student academic success! But, the unbelievable fast pace took a toll on my diabetes. The quick change from leaving a mostly sedentary job to a very active music job soon created problems for me.

My first hypoglycemic episode occurred shortly before the opening night for parents to meet the teachers and administration. I stayed at school after a full teacher work day. My music room was ready, my bulletin board was up, and I was professionally dressed. At about 6:00 PM., after working very hard and fast all day, I ate the dinner I had prepared, rested my head on my desk, and passed out. All the teachers and administration were to meet in my classroom at 6:30 PM. to discuss the plan for opening night. The reading specialist greeted me and I didn't respond. The school nurse was able to get me awake enough to drink some juice. The reading specialist volunteered to drive me home, and I did not participate in the opening night.

My second incident of hypoglycemia occurred at the end of the first six weeks. One of the kindergarten teachers requested my presence at one of her parent-teacher conferences. It was around 4:00 PM. I knew that my blood sugar was low, but thinking I would be in and out of this conference quickly, I did not eat anything. I walked into the conference and the discussion went longer than I had anticipated. At about 4:45 PM., I fell forward and hit the floor from passing out. I can only imagine how that parent must have felt! The kindergarten teacher had a mother who was a type 1 diabetic and knew exactly what to do. 911 was called immediately! In my confused mind, *I thought the 911 rescuers were little green men from Mars coming to take me away!* I passed out again and woke up in a Methodist Hospital Emergency Room. Low blood sugar can affect a diabetic in many ways. I have actually created some of my best music and writing during a low blood sugar of 45. But on this particular day my blood sugar was at a low 19.

It seems as though I was bombarded with multiple episodes of hypoglycemia during the five-and-a-half years I worked in the Lamar C.I.S.D.

I had not learned yet to turn my pump off when a possible low-blood sugar threatened me. Several advanced features on the insulin pump were not yet available for me. One very important feature is that the pump turns off when a low-blood sugar begins. I did not have this feature on my insulin pump. Also, I never could hear my pump alarms in the music classroom. I switched to the pump buzz alarm, but often I was too active to feel it. Sometimes students would tell me when they heard my pump give an alarm.

During my years of teaching in the Lamar C.I.S.D., I passed out three times while teaching. Another time, I passed out after teaching a recorder class after school. The recorder students had left, and I had returned to my classroom to rearrange the chairs and to distribute new music into their storage slots. I found some recorders laying on the floor and reached up to put them in a special place on a high shelf. I had no sooner done this and I passed out. The time was about 5:30 PM., and I didn't awake up until 8:30 PM. What a miracle that I woke up! Thank you Lord Jesus. I stumbled across my classroom to my desk and ate some glucose tablets immediately. Totally exhausted, I drove to my apartment, ate supper, got my shower, and collapsed into bed.

I was living alone in my apartment, and this was not a good choice. Paul was able to join me later. In the meantime, I passed out once in the apartment after hauling my groceries up a flight of stairs. Again, I woke up hours later at the foot of my bed. I believe God had sent my guardian angel once again to watch over me.

I only mentioned the most significant incidences of low-blood sugar during my years with the Lamar C.I.S.D. There were many more passing out or near passing out medical emergencies. Every single time, my Lord Jesus made sure I was well cared for. I would be willing to speculate that when I retired from teaching, many of my guardian angels requested retirement also. No kidding, I am going to hug all my guardian angels when I get to heaven!

My years with the Lamar C.I.S.D. were the best years in my teaching career. I was still in the district when I retired from teaching on January 15, 2012. In January of 2011, I had begun working on my doctorate in educational leadership. I was able to obtain an A average on the first six hours I completed. But, the stress and the inability to get a student loan were too much. I could not afford to pay out-of-pocket again. For me, doing those six hours were very meaningful.

I would love to teach elementary music education at Texas A.&M., Corpus Christi. If the Lord wants me to do this, then He will open that door.

Chapter 20

Teacher Retirement on January 15, 2012

The day of my teacher retirement had finally arrived. I could hardly imagine it, let alone experience it! Believe me, it is *a dream afar off* for most teachers. I had just experienced the best teaching of my career. The Elementary Music Specialists in the Lamar C.I.S.D. were a very close-knit professional team of educators. We depended upon one another often for borrowed classroom supplies, demonstration of successful teaching strategies, and joint curriculum planning. These music teachers were absolutely awesome! We were more than twenty in number as many new elementary schools had been built in the Lamar School District. I had learned much from them, and I am very glad to have been a part of their network. Several of these teachers came to my retirement ceremony at Hutchinson Elementary School and honored me with their gifts and cards. My own teaching team at Hutchinson Elementary School honored me with a gorgeous retirement teacher's plaque with a baton and a golden soprano recorder flute attached. It made me very very happy! This was a very joyful ending to a wonderful teaching career. It is always hard to say goodbye to the co-workers you have worked with so closely. Paul had to do the same at the school he was teaching in. The next day, we were headed back to Corpus Christi.

Chapter 21

God's Wonderful Family

God's children are everywhere! If you have been born again, you are God's child, and you are a member of the family of God. As a minister of music, I have met and fellow-shipped with hundreds of people who love and know the Lord Jesus Christ as their personal Savior. In every place that Paul and I have lived, there were always a group of Christians waiting to greet and to help us. I am so glad to be a part of God's universal family. I have also been in denominations outside of the Baptist church. These fellow Christians loved me without reservation, and our fellowship was sweet beyond words.

After I retired as a music teacher, I found a Bible-believing and a Bible-preaching church in Corpus Christi, Texas that I knew God wanted me to be a part of. God spoke to me about joining Southcrest Baptist Church five years before I retired. I joined the church in January of 2012, and I remain a member. Some of its precious members have since died and gone on to glory, but I praise God for the encouragement and the impact they made upon my life.

It is wonderful to know that when my pastor, Brother Buddy Murphrey, preaches, his message will be straight out of the Bible, God's Word, and anointed by the Holy Spirit of God. I am part of a music team that is awesome because we pray for one another, and we seek the empowerment and direction of the Holy Spirit before ministering. Without the power of God's Holy Spirit anointing our music, we would be wasting our time.

All the members and visitors of Southcrest Baptist are my friends for life. Some of these wonderful Christians are prayer intercessors that meet on Wednesday night and kneel at the altar in earnest prayer for the many needs of people. Our pastor preaches an edifying message first from the Bible.

Just a few weeks ago, God used his message entitled *The Ministry of the Thorn* to inspire me to write this book. I have seen many answers to prayer as a result of the intercessory prayer of these prayer warriors. God bless them all very richly.

Chapter 22

A Leap of Faith

Faith healing and faith healers are both very difficult and controversial subjects to openly write or talk about. I had not planned to include this chapter in my book, but I believe God wants me to share with you my experience and the truths he has taught me.

I had visited some nationally known healers throughout the United States. I had been prayed for in Jesus name, anointed with oil, and even slain in the spirit in some places. In every instance, I believed one hundred per cent that I would be healed of diabetes mellitus. A giant leap of faith was initiated in me through the power of God's Holy Spirit.

It is so very easy to take Scripture out of context when teaching or preaching about faith healing. The worst comment you can make to an unhealed person is *they lacked faith in God.* As a born-again child of God, I believe God's healing does continue in this day and age in which we live. I have been healed of ailments both with and without medical intervention. One of the most positive healings I have received is a weight loss of eighty-five pounds. In December of 2017, I began my weight loss journey under Dr. Craig Chang of Victoria, Texas. Through changing my eating habits, consistent exercising at the gym four times a week and gastric sleeve surgery, I've obtained a medical miracle. Months before I even had heard of Dr. Chang, I prayed to God to help me find a way to lose a lot of weight. God used Dr. Chang to bring about this healing. I feel better physically than I ever remember, and my insulin intake has decreased remarkably.

Why haven't I been completely healed of diabetes mellitus? I believe there are several reasons why God hasn't healed me. First, God has used me in the lives of many people to demonstrate the power of his love and his grace.

God's love and grace never runs out! Furthermore, God's strength never runs out!

Paul, who was never healed either, put it this way as he wrote under the inspiration of the Holy Spirit:

And lest I should be exalted above measure through the abundance of the revelations, there was given to me a thorn in the flesh, the messenger of Satan to buffet me, lest I should be exalted above measure. For this thing I besought the Lord thrice, that it might depart from me. And he said unto me, my grace is sufficient for thee: for my strength is made perfect in weakness. Most gladly therefore will I rather glory in my infirmities, that the power of Christ may rest upon me. Therefore, I take pleasure in infirmities, in reproaches, in necessities, in persecutions, in distresses for Christ's sake: for when I am weak, then am I strong. (2 Corinthians 12:7-10, KJV)

Sometimes people are absolutely shocked that I even have type 1 diabetes or that I have had it for over a half-century. God has blessed me with his strength and his never ending peace and joy. I've been able to retain a zeal for living and a desire to reflect God's glory in every way possible. Through my diabetes, I have come to know the unsearchable riches of Christ Jesus. I have come to understand the blessing of each new day, of being able to walk and to talk unhindered, and to not feel inferior because of my disease. I am not a hopeless or useless diabetic, but I am an insulin-dependent person who has come to understand that I can do all things through Christ.

Secondly, I have discovered that not being healed *does not show a lack of faith*, but it builds a greater faith. God absolutely has the power to heal me of type 1 diabetes. He has chosen not to heal me because through His sovereignty and unending grace, I have come to understand greater empathy, purpose in life, dependence upon Him, and more Christ-likeness in my daily walk.

Thirdly, surrendering to people or to situations I find myself in, are not one of my personal strong traits. In an insulin-dependent diabetic, a physical battle wages between high blood sugar and low blood sugar all the time because a balance must be maintained between the two. I have learned to surrender myself into the arms of my blessed Savior, Jesus Christ. God has also taught me very well to listen to and not to resist those trying to help me.

Fourthly, I have had greater power to evangelize. I love to share what God has done in my life. I love to tell others how Jesus Christ saved me at the age of seventeen and turned me completely around. My diabetes becomes a witness of God's unending grace because it testifies of Gods' continued strength, love and watch care over me.

I rejoice whenever I hear of someone receiving a genuine healing miracle. But, I have discovered these authentic healings are but few in number. I have come to realize, as an insulin-dependent diabetic for fifty-four years, that God's internal peace and joy are greater than physical healing. We all live in a physical body that will someday die. We, who know Jesus Christ as our personal Lord and Savior, will then receive ultimate healing instantly from God, our loving and wonderful Heavenly Father.

Our focus of faith should always be upon our great God and Savior, Jesus Christ. Jesus' priority was upon preaching the gospel. Healing was secondary. If you have been to famous faith healers and stood in numerous healing lines, don't be too hard on yourself for not receiving your healing. God has a greater purpose for you! It is to get born-again if you have not done so already.

Chapter 23

Do You Know Your Eternal Destiny?

Do you know where you would spend eternity if you were to die today? This is the most important question you will ever be asked in your lifetime. The Bible makes it very clear that it will be either heaven or hell. Your eternal destiny depends upon your willingness or unwillingness to accept Jesus Christ, God's Son, as your personal Lord and Savior. The Bible tells us that JESUS CHRIST, GOD'S ONLY BEGOTTEN SON, IS THE ONLY WAY TO HEAVEN!

Jesus Christ said so himself in the Book of John as well as throughout the entire Bible. These verses are only a few of many that make this truth very clear.

"For God so loved the world, that he gave his only begotten Son, that whosoever believeth in him should not perish, but have everlasting life." (John 3:16, KJV)

"Herein is love, not that we loved God, but that He loved us, and sent His Son to be the propitiation (atoning sacrifice) for our sins." (1 John 4:10, KJV)

"For the wages of sin is death; but the gift of God is eternal life through Jesus Christ our Lord." (Romans 6:23, KJV)

"I, even I, am the LORD, And there is no savior besides Me." (Isaiah 43:11 KJV)

"Jesus saith unto him, I am the way, the truth, and the life: no man cometh unto the Father, but by me." (John 14:6, KJV)

One thousand years before the birth of Jesus Christ, David wrote a very detailed account of Jesus Christ dying on the Cross for our sins. It is Psalm 22. God loves us so much that he sent Jesus Christ, his only begotten Son, to make full payment for all your sins and for mine. The apostle Peter gives us a dramatic picture of God's love for us and of Christ's payment for our sin:

"Forasmuch as ye know that ye were not redeemed with corruptible things, as silver and gold, from your vain conversation received by tradition from your fathers; but with the precious blood of Christ, as of a lamb without blemish and without spot . . . " (1 Peter 1:18,19, KJV)

I cringe every time I hear someone refer to my Christian faith as a religion. Religion is man reaching up to God through self-effort in hopes of going to heaven after death. Christianity is God reaching down to man and freely offering a *know so salvation from* hell's eternal damnation. We cannot save ourselves because Jesus Christ has fully paid our debt of sin with His own precious blood.

On the third day, after Jesus Christ died on the cross, God raised him from the dead. Christ's resurrection from the dead is the main doctrine of Christian Biblical faith. It separates Christianity from all the religions of the world.

This proven historical fact od A.D, affirms everything the scriptures say about Christ's resurrection. A few non christian philosophies and religions have unproven claims of their leaders being resurrected. Without the resurrection, all that I have shared with you about Jesus Christ, would be a big and deceptive lie!

"Jesus said unto her, I am the resurrection, and the life: he that believeth in me, though he were dead, yet shall he live: And whosoever liveth and believeth in me shall never die..." (John 11:25,26, KJV)

"Blessed be the God and Father of our Lord Jesus Christ, which according to his abundant mercy hath begotten us again unto a lively hope by the resurrection of Jesus Christ from the dead, to an inheritance incorruptible, and undefiled, and that fadeth not away, reserved in heaven for you..." (1 Peter 1:3,4, KJV)

I know I have written about many verses in the Bible. The Bible is what God's Holy Spirit uses to convict a sinner of their need of salvation.

"For the word of God is quick, and powerful, and sharper than any two-edged sword, piercing even to the dividing asunder of soul and spirit, and of the joints and marrow, and is a discerner of the thoughts and intents of the heart. (Hebrews 4:12, KJV)

You may be thinking about the Lord Jesus Christ right now. You may be thinking that just by believing everything I have said is good enough to get you into heaven. That would be an intellectual belief and not a born-again experience. You would die and go straight to hell after death. Receiving Christ into your heart is like a type 1 diabetic taking insulin. I can look at a bottle of insulin and say, "I believe everything my doctor has told me about my need to take this insulin to prevent my physical death." But, to intellectually believe in insulin without actually taking it would lead to your physical death. You have to receive or inject yourself with insulin in order to live. Likewise, you have to receive the Lord Jesus Christ into your heart in order to be born again and have a new life in Him. To reject Him is eternal death! Please read this last verse aloud.

"Behold, I stand at the <u>door</u>, (your heart and your life) and <u>knock</u> (Jesus does this): if any man (or woman) <u>hear my voice</u> (this is the Holy Spirit telling you of your need to accept Jesus Christ), and <u>open the door</u> (only you can open the door), I will <u>come in</u> to him (Jesus is speaking directly to you), and will <u>sup</u> (Jesus will fellowship with us in an awesome, personal, and communicative manner) with him, and he with me. (Revelation 3:20, KJV)

Is the Lord Jesus knocking on your heart's door right now? If so, this is the moment for you to be born again. *(… Behold, now is the accepted time; behold, now is the day of salvation - 2 Corinthians 6:2, KJV)*. Pray to the Lord Jesus right now and tell him you know you are a hell-bound sinner and that you know he shed His precious blood to cleanse you from all your sin. Ask Him to come into your heart and to help you do his will each day. Speak from the very depth of your heart and mean it.

If you accepted the Lord Jesus Christ as your Personal Savior, find yourself a good Bible-believing, evangelical church to attend. Share with the pastor what has happened to you. Buy yourself a King James Bible and begin reading it every day. Remember that the Bible is not a novel, so I recommend you don't begin with Genesis, the first book in the Old Testament. Start with Romans, the Gospel of John, Ephesians, or any of the books of the Bible from which I have used verses. Always pray for the Holy Spirit, who now indwells you, to guide you in your understanding of Scripture. Stay in fellowship with godly Christians who love our Lord Jesus Christ and the Bible. Make prayer a special time during your day. But, most of all, walk with Jesus in your new found faith. None of these suggestions have anything to do with you either getting born-again of staying born-again. That matter has already been settled forever! You are about to discover and journey into God's awesome and unending grace! Amen and amen!

The End

About the Author

Pamela Diane Worley was born in the small, thriving coal-mining town of Iaeger, WV on January 15,1950. Her mother taught in the local elementary school, and her father sold insurance. Pamela's childhood was remarkable. She was very successful academically and musically. She graduated as an honor student in high school and began a major in music education in college soon afterwards. In 1972, she graduated with a B.S. in Secondary Education from Bob Jones University in Greenville, SC. She taught for three years in a private Christian Academy in Corpus Christi, Texas. There, she met and married Paul I. Worley, an active duty Coast Guardsman. Over the next few years, they moved to several locations in the United States, and became parents to two boys and one adopted Korean daughter.

In 1993, Pamela began her professional teaching career in public school as an elementary music Specialist. She retired in January of 2012 at the age of 62. During her teaching career, she earned two Master Degrees in School Counseling and in Educational Curriculum and Instruction from Texas A&M University, Corpus Christi. She also pursued a Doctorate in Educational Leadership. In addition, she earned $12,000 for her elementary music classroom through successful writing educational grants.

Pamela has also been an active Minister of Music in churches across the United States. She is presently a Minister of Music at a local Baptist Church in Corpus Christi, Texas. Pamela enjoys her family, her two grandchildren, and her two cats. She loves people and has never known a stranger in her entire life.